WISE WORDS

CHARLI XCX

AN UNOFFICIAL QUOTE BOOK

COMPILED BY MILLIE ACERS

CONTENTS

DISCLAIMER

This book has in no way been written or endorsed by Charli xcx. It was created by Angels, for Angels. It is a love letter to Charli and all those who are inspired by her and feel a connection to her music.

INTRODUCTION

At the end of 2024, Charli xcx posted her "manifesto" for *brat*, dated summer 2023. She wrote, "This is Global. I will provide the momentum and tell the story in a laser-focused way. We must execute everything with power and confidence." The manifesto was so prophetic that some even questioned its validity, because she predicted with biting specificity the rollout, the reception, and the *brat* universe that took the world by storm.

But it wasn't a prediction; it was all by design. *brat* unfolded in the way that it did because Charli has always committed so completely to the world-building of all her albums. If she was determined to "cultivate desire, chaos, and destruction", that's exactly what she would do.

There is so much more to Charli's artistry than this breakout record, which has taken her from the fringes of pop stardom to new mainstream heights. Her early years were full of musical experimentation, as she struggled to carve out a space that felt uniquely "her". Songs such as 'I Love It' with Icona Pop in 2012, 'Fancy' with Iggy Azalea and 'Boom Clap' from *The Fault in Our Stars* soundtrack in 2014 all pushed her further into the limelight. You can hear what would become Charli signatures radiating through

› › › › › › › › › › ›

these tracks, from the braggadocious lyricism to the synth-pop sensibilities. But it wasn't until she dropped 'Vroom Vroom' in 2015 that she fully found her footing. Sonically thrilling and lyrically bold, the track marked the beginning of Charli's trademark sound — and the beginning of her collaboration with production powerhouse SOPHIE, who would become a major influence for Charli, inspiring her heart-wrenching song 'So I'.

Charli's fans, the Angels will argue vehemently over her greatest achievement. Is it the feature-stacked work of art that is the *Pop 2* mixtape? The expansive and explosive *Charli*? The introspective DIY lockdown creation *how i'm feeling now*? Or did *brat* reach such heights because it is her most accomplished album?

Whatever your preference, it is Charli's persona and voice that drives her music. In this book you'll find Charli's unique philosophy for life, in her very own words. Featuring her wisdom on everything from making art to partying, and from finding confidence to growing up, discover Charli at her funniest, bravest, most vulnerable and most outrageous. So grab a white tank top and a Bic lighter, and let's ride!

BACK TO 1999

Charlotte Aitchison was born in 1992 and grew up in a village close to Stansted Airport, around 30 miles north of London. As a teenager, Charli posted religiously to MySpace, where her music caught the attention of an events planner in London. At just 15, Charli was invited to perform at warehouse raves in Hackney, which her understandably anxious parents would take her to. Here she encountered club and queer culture for the first time, something she describes as hugely formative to her entire career. She called herself "Charli xcx" after her MSN Messenger display name and an icon was born.

“

I always felt like a loser. I had friends, but my school was full of blonde white girls and I was this half-Indian girl with frizzy hair and different interests.

”

"[My parents] started from nothing and worked so hard to be able to give themselves a life they loved. Growing up around that has an effect on you."

"When I was seven I was having fun; I was pretending to be Baby Spice, I was obsessed with Britney Spears. That was a pretty good time."

BACK TO 1999

"As a woman in the music industry, when you start really young and you're not really shown the way, it can be really intimidating."

BACK TO 1999

"When you're 16 and you sign [to a record label] and you go through rounds with producers, that kind of factory way where you go in and you meet someone and you do a song and you leave — you don't really know who you are."

"I lived in *Hertfordshire*! I'd never been to a party like this before. I didn't know anything about rave culture, or club-kid culture, or gay culture — everything was a first that night."

PARTY 4 U

Charli is a party girl — it's at the core of everything she does as an artist. She writes about partying with pinpoint specificity, describing the euphoria and pain, the love and loss, the beginning and ending. It's not just about the drinking and overindulgence, it's about the moments of raw connection and vulnerability that happen when you're at a party. Everything is romantic, after all.

PARTY 4 U

“

If you want to get over something you go to a party. If you want to spend time with people that you love, you’re at a party. If you’re young and you meet someone and you fall in love, it’s often at a party. I think it’s an important part of growing up.

”

"Partying is sometimes a really important and cathartic moment for people, but sometimes it can be really lonely."

"Someone tried to sell my dad MDMA, but he thought they said MDF, like the flooring. So he was like, 'Yeah! I don't have any room in my car right now though!'"

PARTY 4 U

"I saw Patrick Wolf throw up in his own hands and eat it at a show once ... I just thought, 'Oh my god, I still fancy you', which was weird."

PARTY 4 U

"I'm not religious at all, but I feel like … if you want to take it there, the club or a party can be a church for somebody. It's like a community of people who are just letting go and being free. It's like gay church."

"Clubs are really fruitful, creative spaces for me. I get inspired lyrically, visually, the whole thing. The light and lasers in clubs or at raves, the space itself. It's very inspiring to me."

BREAK THE RULES

Charli has carved out her own space in the pop world. She doesn't tone down her music or image in order to fit into the mainstream idea of what a popstar is. She leads, and demands her audience follow. PC music, coming in the form of collaborators including A.G. Cook and SOPHIE, has inspired some of her most complex and fascinating music, but it's a far cry from what her label would have expected from a pure popstar. As always, Charli knew that if she kept on putting out music that inspired her, the world would catch up.

BREAK THE RULES

“

Music is not important...
Artistry is important, and some artists don’t have artistry.
I need an artist to create the world. A great artist to me is more than the songs, it’s the entire culture and space that they inhabit.

”

"Now niche is rewarded so much more than it ever has been and I think that record labels recognise that."

"'Vroom Vroom' is the Regina George of my songs. She's bitchy, she's sassy, people love her, she goes hard, she's hot and she f***s s*** up."

BREAK THE RULES

"I enjoy poking fun at [pop music]. I enjoy buying into it, believing it, rejecting it, being a mess and the chaos within it."

BREAK THE RULES

"I have no interest in working with someone just because they're the new hot s***. I have interest in working with people who inspire me and people I think could make an impact on pop culture and the way music sounds, and that's what I see with PC Music."

"I feel most comfortable in the studio. You don't have to put makeup on, you don't have to dress up or think or care about what anyone thinks of you. You can just go."

"Now every single move is considered... I think about every element of my artistry so in-depth that I feel truly *potent* now."

“Playing in those more underground environments and being exposed to fashion and LGBTQ+ culture — that was the first time I felt truly inspired to my core. It was like I’d opened Pandora’s box.”

FAMOUS

Fame is complex, and one thing Charli makes clear is that under all the bravado, she's still a sensitive person with her own issues and insecurities. For most of her career she's been beloved, but not necessarily an A-lister. She has found her largest and most devoted audience in the club and queer scenes. The fanbase that has gravitated towards her seems to be the fanbase that she finds the most solace and freedom in. Her collaborative lockdown album *how i'm feeling now* was a direct conversation with her fans, created with and for them.

“

I’ve always been caught in this dichotomy of ‘Am I a left-field underground artist or am I supposed to be a popstar?’

”

"I think fame is fun and an interesting medium to operate within. You can treat it in a very Warholian kind of way and play games with it."

FAMOUS

"In the public eye, I feel like you have these moments where you're like, 'I'm on top of the world, I'm the best, no one can touch me', and then literally 24 hours later you can be like, 'I hate myself, no one cares about what I'm doing, what's the point?'"

"I find it difficult to deal with someone who rejects me and then kisses my ass later — even though I know that's what the whole music industry *is*."

"I've seen a lot of commentary [online] of 'She's taken it too far — she really has sold out!' But people who take it too far are better than people who don't. I don't want to feel safe in the hands of musicians I admire, I want to feel like: f***, I don't know what they're going to do next."

"I don't even see myself as a popstar. I see myself as an anti-popstar."

"A lot of gay men like my music. It is a fact. I'm sorry, but I'm claiming that."

“

My LGBTQ+ audience believed in me when nobody else really did, and I think they really understood me at a point in time when everybody else was confused or unconvinced by me. They gave me a lot of confidence to express myself and feel comfortable in my own skin.

”

FAMOUS

"I kinda miss the time when pop music was really volatile and crazy. I miss the Paris Hilton days. Everybody is so worried about everything right now — how they're perceived, if this art they've created is going to offend anyone."

"I am a role model for a very flawed, genuinely real, non-perfect person. And that's all I would ever want to be."

"Strange things have been thrown on stage. I've gotten someone's mum's ashes in a jar."

FAMOUS

"Out of everything I've done in my whole career ... my name being in *EastEnders* is the thing that most people in my life, personally and online, are most excited about... They're most excited about the fact that Stacey Slater's grandchild is named after me."

GIRL, SO CONFUSING

While other artists make diss tracks, Charli opted for something much more nuanced and radical with 'Girl, so confusing'. Rather than attacking the subject of her song, she talks about the confusion and complexities of relationships between women, especially between competitors pitted against each other. Charli has always been a feminist, but she also doesn't shy away from the more contentious aspects of womanhood. Lorde's verse on the remix is electric, and the bravery of this frank conversation was felt around the world. The Internet did, in fact, go crazy.

“

Someone I continuously get asked about is Lorde. People love to pin us up against each other. I don’t give a f***. I admire her greatly: she is so prolific and so kind, and is such a talent for the younger generation. It’s so cool that she has such a platform.

”

"If you don't like all other women who exist and breathe on this Earth then you're a bad feminist. If you're not a girl's girl then you're a bad woman."

GIRL, SO CONFUSING

"People were like, 'Oh, who wrote your songs?' There's so much doubt, especially with being a popstar and being a female. Taylor Swift: *amazing* songwriter. Katy Perry: *amazing* songwriter. Lady Gaga: *amazing* songwriter."

"Being a woman is so nuanced and complex all the time, let alone through the lens of a very male-focused industry like the music industry."

"[The music industry is] really competitive, and it's really hard sometimes. The media does it to us, labels do that to us, the narrative around being a woman does that to us."

> "Relationships between women are super complex and multi-layered. You can like someone and dislike them at the same time; you can feel jealous of somebody but they can still be your friend; you can have the best time of your life on a night out with someone, but not be that close to them at all."

"SOPHIE was really instrumental in encouraging me to just go with my gut."

GIRL, SO CONFUSING

"I'll always think SOPHIE is the future. She, to me, is just such a groundbreaking producer, so special and unique in the way she creates sounds and writes songs."

BRAT

From Kamala Harris to the *Collin's Dictionary* word of the year, the pop culture phenomenon that was *brat* cannot be overstated. Yet in all the *brat* summer antics, it's easy to lose sight of how good the actual music is. In this diary of a party girl, we move through the ecstasy of the dancefloor, to meditations on Charli's deepest insecurities, to a moving tribute to SOPHIE, to a reflection on intergenerational trauma, to brutal reckonings with the reality of having children, then right back to the dancefloor. It captured the zeitgeist in a way that's incomparable — the perfect album at the perfect time. She *is* so Julia.

> "Like, when Martha [Stewart] gets mad about an old magazine article and says she's glad the journalist who wrote it is dead — that is *brat*. And then when that exact journalist responded and said, 'Hey! I'm alive, bitch!' — that is extremely *brat*."

"A pack of cigs, and a Bic lighter, and a strappy white top with no bra… That's kind of all you need."

"If I was writing a song with A.G. Cook or Cirkut, it would just immediately be like, 'That's not *brat*,' and we would move on and do something that was *brat*."

"The world is inspired by dancing at a rave and being really sweaty with your nipples showing through a tank top more than it is by an artist."

"I wanted to create this world of that 2000s flip phone, cameras flashing, live fast, die young. I wanted my lyrics to be conversational because that's what I think pop culture actually is. It's a 15-second TikTok, a selfie in a cloud, a text to your friends being like 'Where you at, b****?'"

"The *brat* green ... there's kind of this idea of taking something quite disgusting and turning it into this thing you know people are gonna look at quite a lot... I really enjoyed that some people really hated it."

Penguin Random House

Editors Millie Acers and Lara Hutcheson
Custom Designer Catherine Holmes
Senior Production Editor Jennifer Murray
Senior Production Controller Louise Minihane
Art Director Jo Connor
Managing Director Mark Searle
Written by Millie Acers

First published in Great Britain in 2025 by Doring Kindersley Limited
20 Vauxhall Bridge Road, London SW1V 2SA.
The authorised representative in the EEA is Dorling Kindersley Verlag GmbH. Arnulfstr. 124, 80636 Munich, Germany.
First American edition, 2025
Published in the United States by DK Publishing, 1745 Broadway, 20th Floor, New York, NY 10019

25 26 27 28 29 30 10 9 8 7 6 5 4 3 2 1
001–355106–May/2025

A CIP catalogue record for this book is available from the British Library.
A catalog record for this book is available from the Library of Congress.
ISBN: 978-0-2417-8012-1
Printed and bound in China
www.dk.com

Quotations: p.4 "Brat Manifesto", *Pop Crave*, 2024 **p.8** "Charli XCX is too real", *GQ*, Jeff Weis, 2024; **p.9** "Charli XCX: 'It's weird yelling into a mic while my boyfriend does a puzzle'", *The Guardian*, Laura Snapes, 2020; **p.10** "Charli XCX Tells Us About "1999," Her Glossy New Troye Sivan Collab", *Vice*, Shaad D'Souza, 2018; **p.11** "Charli XCX 'BRAT' Confessions While Taking You Through A Day In Her Life", *Billboard*, 2024; **p.12** "Shame Less", *FADER*, Duncan Cooper, 2015; **p.13** "Charli XCX: 'Every single thing is work for me. Everything is music'", *The Guardian*, Tom Lamount, 2018; **p.16** "2017: The Year Pop Finally Caught Up To Charli XCX", *Vice*, Emma Garland, 2017; **p.17** "Charli XCX Gets Extremely Real About Her Mixtape And New Music", *FADER*, Owen Myers, 2017; **p.18** "'Someone tried to sell my dad MDMA' – Charli XCX Interview on Starting Out on the Rave Scene", *ITN*, Jasmin Dotiwala, 2014; **p.19** "Charli XCX Doesn't Care For Your Misogynistic Bullshit", *Vice*, Alex Donovan, 2012; **p.20–21** "It's Charli XCX's Party—And Everyone's Invited", *Glamour*, Christopher Rosa, 2019; **p.24** "Episode 95: @charli_xcx says music is not important", *Subway Takes*, Kareem Rahma, 2024; **p.25** "Charli xcx: The BRAT Interview", *Apple Music*, Zane Lowe, 2024; **p.26** "Charli XCX Takes a Love Language Quiz", *PAPER*, 2019; **p.27** "Charli XCX: 'I like playing games with pop music. I enjoy poking fun at it'", *NME*, El Hunt, 2022; **p.28** "2017: The Year Pop Finally Caught Up To Charli XCX", *Vice*, Emma Garland, 2017; **p.29** "Charli XCX on Her New Mixtape and Why She's Not Sure She'll Release Another Album", *Vulture*, Dee Lockett, 2017; **p.30** "'Brat' Unfiltered: Charli xcx on How She Stole the Summer (And Worked It Out With Lorde on the Remix)", *Billboard*, Kristin Robinson, 2024; **p.31** "Charli XCX: 'It's weird yelling into a mic while my boyfriend does a puzzle'", *The Guardian*, Laura Snapes, 2020; **p.34** "Charli xcx: The BRAT Interview", *Apple Music*, Zane Lowe, 2024; **p.35** "The Howard Stern Show 10/02/2024 Charli xcx", *The Howard Stern Show*, Howard Stern, 2024; **p.36** "Charli XCX: Therapuss with Jake Shane", 2024; **p.37** "Interview: Charli XCX", *Pitchfork*, Jill Mapes, 2014; **p.38** "Charli XCX: 'People who take it too far are better than people who don't'", *The Guardian*, Rachel Aroesti, 2022; **p.39** "'Someone tried to sell my dad MDMA' – Charli XCX Interview on Starting Out on the Rave Scene", *ITN*, Jasmin Dotiwala, 2014; **p.40** "'It's A Secret!' Charli XCX Answers The Internet", *Hits Radio*, 2023; **p.41** "Charli XCX Joins Brittany Broski's Royal Court", *Royal Court*, Brittany Broski, 2024; **p.42–43** "Charli XCX knows you're obsessed with her", *The Face*, Shaad D'Souza, 2024; **p.44** "Charli XCX on how to have the ultimate Brat summer", *BBC Sounds*, Nick Grimshaw and Annie Mac, 2024; **p.45** "'It's A Secret!' Charli XCX Answers The Internet", *Hits Radio*, 2023; **p.48** "Interview: Charli XCX", *Pitchfork*, Jill Mapes, 2014; **p.49** "Charli XCX: 'Labels are desperate for artists to be liked, otherwise you're bad, evil and wrong'", *The Guardian*, Kate Mossam, 2024; **p.50** "Halsey and Charli XCX, Fall's Wildest Tourmates, Talk Partying, Sexism and Songwriting: 'We're Helping Each Other Win'", *Billboard*, Brooke Mazurek, 2017; **p.51** "Charli XCX Accepts the Powerhouse Award", *Billboard*, 2024; **p.52** "Charli XCX Accepts the Powerhouse Award", *Billboard*, 2024; **p.53** "Charli XCX: 'Labels are desperate for artists to be liked, otherwise you're bad, evil and wrong'", *The Guardian*, Kate Mossam, 2024; **p.54** "Charli xcx on BRAT and her life in club culture", *RA Exchange*, Chal Ravens, 2024; **p.55** "Charli XCX Tells Us About "1999," Her Glossy New Troye Sivan Collab", *Vice*, Shaad D'Souza, 2018; **p.58** "Charli xcx Monologue 16/11/2024", *Saturday Night Live*, 2024; **p.59** "Charli XCX on how to have the ultimate Brat summer", *BBC Sounds*, Nick Grimshaw and Annie Mac, 2024; **p.60** "Charli xcx on the Year of the 'Brat,' Advice From Ariana Grande and Pivoting to Acting: 'I'm at This Crossroad'", *Variety*, Jem Aswad, 2024; **p.61** "Charli xcx on BRAT and her life in club culture", *RA Exchange*, Chal Ravens, 2024; **p.62** "Charli XCX is too real", *GQ*, Jeff Weis, 2024; **p.63** "Charli XCX 'BRAT' Confessions While Taking You Through A Day In Her Life", *Billboard*, 2024

FSC www.fsc.org
MIX
Paper | Supporting responsible forestry
FSC™ C018179

This book was made with Forest Stewardship Council™ certified paper – one small step in DK's commitment to a sustainable future.

Learn more at www.dk.com/uk/information/sustainability